*Finger Plays & Action Verses
For Concept Reinforcement*

By Ruth I. Dowell
Illustrations by Pete Johnson

Pollyanna Expanded Version ©1997

For a list of other books
by Ruth and/or to schedule
her workshop, contact:

Pollyanna Productions
P O Box 3222 • Terre Haute, IN 47803-0222
(800) 257-3286

©1997 (Expanded Edition) Ruth I. Dowell
Published and Distributed by
Pollyanna Productions
All Rights Reserved
Printed in the U.S.A.

Introduction

BENDING! TWISTING! TURNING! GESTURING! Meaningful movement involving motor skills reinforces language patterns and is, therefore, especially helpful in teaching basic concepts to young children. That it is, also, FUN to move about and experience the physical self should not be overlooked. These rhymes, easy-to-learn and easy-to-say-and-do, have been "kid-tested and approved" by hundreds of children nationwide. It is with great pleasure that we, therefore, present these patterns for **FITNESS, FUN AND FUNDAMENTALS.**

Best wishes for happy times,

Ruth I. Dowell
Children's Poet/Author

Note: Multiple concepts on every page.

Concept Reference

Action Words
Two Good Thumbs 9
What Can You Do? 13
Rub It In! 16
Johnny Jump Jump 18
The Rocking Chair 20
Dicky Ducky 26
If I Just Pretend 27
See Me Move 30
Snap Your Fingers 31
Up On Your Toes 33

Adjectives
What Am I? 28
Draw a Picture 36

Analogies
What Can You Do? 13

Body Awareness
Touch a Finger 10
I Have Ears To Hear With 15
Rub It In! 16
Body Talk 17
Make an "X" 24
Hang Your Head Down Low 25
I'm Made That Way 41
Feet & Ankles 43

Cause & Effect
Smoke Goes Up 40

Comparatives
Drawing Circles 38

Numbers
Left Side! Right Side! 14
Up On Your Toes (using 1,2,3,4 instead of l/r, l/r) 33

Position Words
Shrug Your Shoulders 6
Draw a Circle 8
Clap Your Hands 11
Sing a Song Together 19
There Go the Raindrops 21
Speedy "Automobeely" 22
Right Foot Forward 23
Hang Your Head Down Low 25
Up the Ladder 29
See Me Move 30
Down the Track 32
Up On Your Toes 33
Hands In the Air 34
Marching, Marching! 37
One Hand Left 39
Smoke Goes Up 40
Wink, Wink, Blink 44

Seasons
Smoke Goes Up 40
Draw a Picture 36

Senses
I Have Ears To Hear With 15

Shapes
Make an "X" 24
Draw a Picture 36

SKILLS: Listening, Following Directions, Group Behaviour and Gross & Fine Motor, etc. *THROUGHOUT!*

A gnat is what I'm glad I'm NOT!
A flea I would not be.
A butterfly? Oh, no; not I.
I'm busy BEE-ing ME!

Table Of Contents

Introduction 3
Concepts/Skills 4
Shrug Your Shoulders 6
I Could Be an Airplane 7
Draw a Circle 8
Two Good Thumbs 9
Touch a Finger 10
Clap Your Hands 11
Open Your Eyes 12
What Can You Do? 13
Left Side! Right Side! 14
I Have Ears To Hear With .. 15
Rub It In! 16
Body Talk 17
Johnny Jump Jump 18
Sing a Song 19
The Rocking Chair 20
There Go the Raindrops ... 21
Speedy Automobeely 22
Right Foot Forward 23

Rub It Out! 24
Hang Your Head Down Low 25
Dicky Ducky 26
If I Just Pretend 27
What Am I? 28
Up the Ladder 29
See Me Move 30
Snap Your Fingers 32
Down the Track 33
Put Your Hands In the Air .. 34
Galloping, Galloping 35
Draw a Picture 36
Marching, Marching 37
Drawing Circles 38
One Hand Left 39
Smoke Goes Up 40
Feet and Ankles 41
Tiptoe, Tiptoe Quietly 42
I'm Made That Way 43
Wink, Wink, Blink! 44

Concepts: Up, down
　　　　　　 Left, right
　　　　　　 Around

Shrug Your Shoulders

(Both shoulders)   **Shrug your shoulders**
                                         Up and down,
(Up/down left; up/down right)   Left and right
(Roll both shoulders)   And all around.

(Extend arms)   Shake your fingers!
(Lift and shake each leg)   Shake your toes!
(Hands on hips)   Now, we're ready.
(Clap on ''here goes!'')   Now, here goes!

Concepts: Straight, wavy
Big
Shapes (circle, triangle)

I Could Be An Airplane

(Hold arms out and soar)   **I could be an airplane!**
(Turn big steering wheel)   I could be a truck!
(Hold arms out and flap wings)   I could be a bi...g bird!
(Tuck fingers into arm pits,
  stoop and "waddle" in a circle)   I could be a duck!

(Touch fingertips overhead)   I could be a sailboat.
(Up/down wave motions with hands)   I could be the sea.
(Extend both arms to show length)   I could be a wha...le.
(Both hands on chest)   But, I'd rather be ME!

Concepts: Circle
In, out
Forward, back
Numbers

Draw a Circle
(Action can take place in a large circle or in a row)

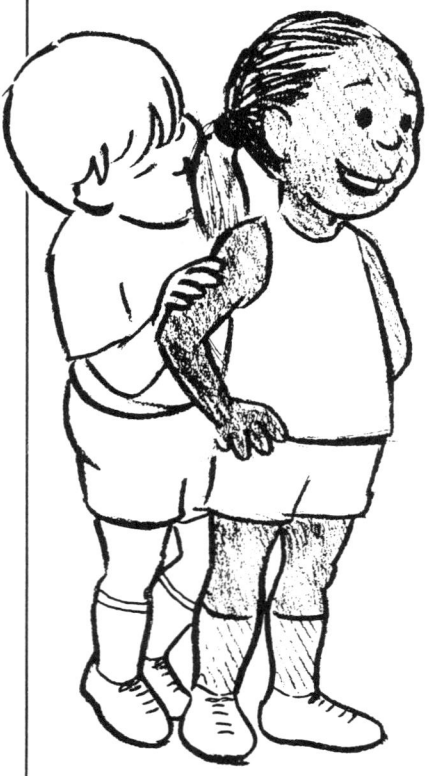

(Each child "draws" circles on floor in front of himself.)   **Draw a circle.**
Jump right in!
Ready, now?
(Jump backwards "out of circle")   Jump out again!
(Slowly...)   Take a step...
or two...or three.
(Shuffle backwards)   Now, back up
And stand with me.

Concepts:	Up & down
	Left & right
Skills:	Point & wave
	Grasping
	Wiggle

Two Good Thumbs
(Tune: "99 Bottles...")

(Both thumbs pointed up) **Thumbs go up and thumbs go down**
(Point left left, point right right) Thumbs go left and right.
(Wiggle thumbs) Thumbs can wiggle just before
(Interlock thumbs) They grab and hold on tight.

(Stamp palms, then thumbs inside) Thumbs can stamp and thumbs can hide.
(Point & motion with thumb) Thumbs can point and wave.
(Thumb & forefinger together) Thumbs can help you pick up things;
("Thumb" nose) But thumbs can *misbehave!*

(Hold up both thumbs) It seems I need my two good thumbs
(Shrug shoulders, palms up) No matter what I do.
(Wiggle fingers) My fingers say, and I agree:
(Forefinger to left thumb; We're glad for you...
  then right) *And you!*

Concepts: Touch
"Shhhh" (Quiet)
Finger/Thumb

Touch a Finger

(Right forefinger touch left forefinger)   **Touch a finger.**
(Right forefinger touch left thumb)   Touch a thumb.
(Touch lips)   Touch the lips that let you *hummm*.
(Side of forefinger to lips)   Now, go *"Shhhh."* That means, *"Be still."*
(Nod head)   Nod your head. That means you will.

Concepts: Off, on
Skills: Listening
Following Directions

Clap Your Hands!

(Clap where underlined)   **Clap your hands <u>like this</u>!**

(Out front, finger pointed)   Hold your arm like this.
Close your eyes!
Keep 'em closed...:
(With pointed finger)   Touch your nose; don't miss!

(One hand overhead/one behind back)   Put your hands like this.
(Quickly, turn completely around)   Turn around like this.
(Hat "off" and back "on")   Tip your hat.
(Sweep arm down across waist)   Take a bow.
(Use both hands)   Throw a great big kiss!

12

Concepts: Up, out
Skills: Dressing self

Open Your Eyes

(Start with eyes closed) **Open your eyes, little sleepy head.**
(Look at wrist watch) Time to get up and get out of bed!
You must get ready for school right now!
(Show steps in dressing) Can you get dressed? Then, show me how!

Concept: Analogies
Tools

What Can You Do?

(Teacher says:)   *(Children say and act out:)*

With a shovel...   *"I can dig."*
With a ball...   *"I can throw."*
With a hammer...   *"I can pound."*
With a boat...   *"I can row."*

With a spoon...   *"I can stir."*
With a broom...   *"I can sweep."*
With a ladder...   *"I can climb."*
With a bed...   *"I can sleep!"*

Concepts: Left/Right
Front/Back
Four

Left Side! Right Side!

(Drop left arm from shoulder height)	**Left side!**
(Drop right arm likewise)	**Right side!**
(Arms at sides)	Have you any more?
(Hands on chest)	Front side!
(Hands on behind)	Back side!
(Hold up four fingers)	That makes four!
(Hands repeat positions quickly)	1-2-3-4!
(Hold up four fingers)	Four!
(Cross wrists; move hands l/r)	No more!

Concepts: Five Senses

I Have Ears To Hear With

(Hands cupped behind ears) **I have ears to hear with.**
(Shade eyes with hand) And I have eyes to see.
(Touch fingertips and rub) Fingers touch and fingers feel.
(Run hands the length of body) They're all a part of me.

(Point to tongue) With my tongue I taste the things
(Rub tummy) I always like to eat.
Some are salty; some are not.
And others sour or sweet.

(Point to nose) With my nose I smell a rose
Or popcorn in a pan.
(Point to each sensory organ) Smell it, hear it, see it, feel it,
(Rub tummy) Taste it. Yes, I can!

Concepts: Body Parts
Action Words (Verbs)

Rub It In!

(Children sitting)

Start giving directions slowly and gradually speed up to the last command. Repeat.

(Both Hands)	**Hold your head!**
(Both Hands)	Touch your toes!
(Both Hands)	Cover your ears!
(Left Hand)	Pinch your nose!
(Both Hands)	Hide your eyes!
(Right Hand)	Grab your chin!
(Left Hand)	Kiss your hand!
(Right Hand)	*Rub it in!*

Concepts: Body Awareness
Skills: Gross Motor (Bending, twisting, turning)

Body Talk

(Tap shoulders four times) **Tap me on my shoulders!**
(Right, right, right)   Slap me on my knee.
(Two times each) Pat my cheeks and scratch my head.
(Put fingers on top of head   Turn me carefully.
and turn around)

(With hands on hips, bend forward) Bend me in the middle.
   Twist me side-to-side.
(Hug self) Use my arms to hug me.
   Stretch them open wide.

(Palms together) Put my hands together.
(Interlock fingers)   Slide my fingers through.
Hold them out in front of me.
(Release fingers and clap twice)   Clap! One, two!

Skills: Gross Motor (Jumping, hopping)

Johnny Jump Jump

(Boys jump in place on both feet seven times)

Jolly Johnny Jump Jump
Coming down the street!
Here comes Holly Hop Hop.
Wonder if they'll meet?

(Girls hop in place on one foot seven times)

(Girls say...:)
(Boys say...:)
(All say...:)
(In place, all Jump, Hop, Stop on both feet.)

"Hello, Johnny Jump Jump!"
"Hello, Holly Hop!"
"Could we stop and rest a minute!"
Jump! Hop! STOP!

Concepts: Together
Side-by-side
Stand
Circle
Left/Right
Back
Stop, sit, stay

Sing a Song Together

(Tune/rhythm: Sing a Song of Six Pence)

(Children stand in line	**Here we are together.**
side-by-side)	Side-by-side we stand.
(Form circle)	Now, we're in a circle.
(Join hands)	Take your neighbor's hand.
(Circle moves, sliding left,	Moving to the left; then,
together, left, together; then,	Back the other way. (See Variation Below)
right, together, right, together.)	Left, right; left, right.
	Stop!
	Sit!
	Stay!

(Variation: Repeat l/r movement to expand the activity)

Skills: Rocking
Still

The Rocking Chair

(Sit with knees pulled up) **I'm a special kind of chair.**
(Rock with arms around knees) See me rocking, rocking:
(Stop rocking) There!
(Sitting quietly) Now, I'm setting very still.
(Look left & right) Who will come and rock?

(Two children sit feet-to-feet, knees bent, clasping hands and rocking) *"I will!"*

(Option: Change partners)

Concepts: Go, come
Up, Down

There Go the Raindrops
(Children in two lines, facing each other)

(Run fingers from left to right)   **There go the raindrops!**
(Touch fingers overhead)   Here comes the sun!
(Walk in place)   Out come the children,
       One by one.

(Swing arms and rock on feet)   Some on the swingset;
(Slide with hands)   Some on the slide.
       "Jump on the seesaw!"
(Joining hands across,   ...Let's ride!"
  lines alternate stooping)

Concepts: Up, over
In, out
Around, through, under

Speedy "Automobeely"

(Hands together in front)	**Up and over!**
(Hands in, palms down, and out)	In and out!
(Make large circle with one hand)	Around
(Hands together, moving "through")	And through
("Dive" with hands, palms down)	And un-der!
(Hands on hips)	Such a speedy "automobeely!"
(Right finger to temple)	Is it safe?? I won-der!

Concepts: Right, left
Forward, back
Together
Skills: Gross Motor (Hopping)

Right Foot Forward

(Lift feet, as you rock from right to left and reverse) **Right foot forward,** rocking back!
Now, the other one; how's that?!
(Hop forward) Feet together; hop, hop, hop!
(Shuffle backwards) Back, back, back; then, hop, hop, stop!

24

Skills: Fine Motor (Marking)

That's That!

(With right hand...) Make an "X" on your chest.
  Draw a circle 'round your ear.
  Put a dot on your nose.
(Overhead) Clap your hands up here.

(With right finger...) Draw a line from your head
  To your toes and back.
(With circular motion, Rub it out! Rub it out! Rub it out!
head-to-toe; then That's that!
dust palms)

Concepts: Low, high, wide
Around, down, through
Body parts

Hang Your Head Down Low

(With arms at sides, drop chin)   **Hang your head down low.**
        Hold your chin up high.
        Make your face go 'round.
           Yes, you can, if you try!

(Swing arms above head)   Spread your feet this wide.
(Between legs)   Swing your arms down through.
(Feet together)   Grab your knees!
        Grab your hips!
           And your shoulders, too!

26

Concepts: Fast, slow

Dicky Ducky

("Swim" fast, then more slowly)   **Dicky Ducky** in the water,
    Swimming fast - - then s-l-o-w.
"Where's your mother, Dicky Ducky?
    Tell me, if you know."

(Point to Mother Duck)   "Quack!" said Dicky; "there's my mother,
    Resting on the shore,
She is tired, but I am not,
("Swim" again)   So, I shall swim some more!"

Concepts: Visual Imagery

If I Just Pretend

(Hands above head)   See me swaying, bending,
                                          Blowing in the wind.
                                 I can be a tall tree.
                                 If I just pretend.

                                 When the day is cloudy,
(Look up)   Look up in the sky.
(Mime raindrops with fingers)   You can be the raindrops.
                                 So can I.

("Swim" with arms)   Swimming in the water,
                                     If I make a wish,
                                 Then, I'm not a person:
(Move hands like fish swimming)   I'm...a...fish!

                                 Wishing and pretending!
                                       It's a lotta fun.
(Hold hands out in front, palms up)   If you're just pretending,
                                         You can be 'most ANYone!

Concepts: Tactile Awareness

What Am I?

(Teacher)	Long and skinny, round and sharp!
(Children, writing in the air)	*That's a pencil!*
(Teacher)	Make a mark!
(Teacher)	Heavy! Hard! Four corners in all!
(Children, placing hand-over-hand)	*That's a brick bat! Build a wall!*
(Teacher)	Oh, so fluffy, soft and white!
(Children cupping hands)	*That's a cotton ball: feel how light!*
(Teacher)	Small and square and cold and wet!
(Children)	*That's an ice cube!*
(ALL)	**YOU BET!**

Note: For variation, other concrete objects can be added to this list, individual children blindfolded and asked to describe and identify each item.

Concepts: Up, down
Top, bottom

Up the Ladder

(Start from stoop, use hands, climb upward)

(End on tiptoes)

(Gradually, come down)

(Move hands away from body, to indicate, "stop!")

Up the ladder!
Climbing!
Up the ladder to the top!
Down the ladder
To the bottom.
When you get there
STOP!

30

Concepts: Left, right
Throw, catch
Hello, goodbye
Twice
Laugh, cry

See Me Move!

(Step left, while moving left arm out and right arm across body; point forefingers and look left) — **See me move** to the left!

(Reverse above action) — See me move to the right!

(Grab shoulders) — See me grab myself!

(Shake self) — See me hold on tight!

(With two hands, overhead) — See me throw the ball!

("Catch" the ball) — See me catch it, too!

("Bounce" the ball) — See me bounce it twice.

(Underhanded) — Now, I'll pass to you.

(Wave hand left to right, palm out) — See me wave HELLO.

(Wave hand up and down) — See me wave GOODBYE.

(Big smile) — See me laugh when you come.

(Rub fists into eyes) — When you go, see me cry!

Skills:	Snapping fingers
Clapping hands
Jumping rope
Touching toes
Jumping high

Snap Your Fingers

(Snap twice)	**Snap your fingers!**
(Clap twice)	Clap your hands!
(Skip rope)	Skip a rope: Jump high! Jump!
	Drop the rope and touch your toes;
(Jump high in air, arms overhead)	Then, reach up to the sky!

Concepts: Front, back
Left, right

Down the Track

(Left foot and arm, with elbow bent, moving forward. Foot and arm back in "locomotive" motion")

Toes in front; then,
pull them back!

(Right foot and arm, with elbow bent, moving forward, then back, as above.

(Repeat movement to the end, where child will pull down on train whistle with the word, "LOUD")

Take that engine
down the track!
If you want to
please the crowd,
blow that engine
whistle LOUD!
Woo! Woo!

Concepts: Up, down
Back and forth
Short, tall
Left, right

Up on Your Toes

Up on your toes and
Down on your heels!
Rock back and forth and
See how it feels!

Now, bend your knees and
Jump up tall!

Left, right! Left, right! Stop!
That's all!

(Pat upper legs, saying:, "left, right, left, right;" or, for variation: "one, two, three, four, five...")

("Hands up on "Stop!")

("Clap on "That's all!")

Concepts: Up, down
Left, right

Hands in the Air!

(Follow directions)   Put your hands in the air.
    Swing 'em down to the ground.
Put 'em right back up.
    Turn around! Turn around!

Bend yourself to the left;
    To the right side, too.
Put your hands on your hips:
    Clap your hands!

(Clap on "can do!")   "CAN DO!"

Concepts: Slow, slower, STOP!

Galloping, Galloping!

(Move in a circle)   **Galloping, galloping!** Here I go!
Riding my horse in the rodeo!
High in the saddle and
   holding on tight!

(Pace words appropriately)   Slow down, there! Slower, now.
   STOP! That's right!

Concepts: Adjectives
Skill: Drawing
Perspective

Draw a Picture

(Move forefingers away from each other, down and back together to form a square; then, same motion, small, for window)
(Spread arms wide)

(Start arms low and raise high)

Draw a house. Make it *square*.
   Draw a window. Make it *small*.
Draw a yard. Make it *wide*.
   Draw a tree. Make it *tall*.

(Draw a long line with finger.)
(Hold arms in a circle)

(Wiggle fingers low to high)

Draw a sidewalk. Make it *long*.
   Draw the sun. Make it *round*.
Draw the flowers in the spring
   Coming out of the ground.

Concepts: Fast, slow
Beside (side-by-side)
High
Counting

Marching, Marching!

(Children in columns, with arms straight down)

Marching, marching! Two by two!
Side by side, as soldiers do!
Steady, now; not fast, not slow.
Stay beside me, as we go!

Lift your knees and bring them high.
We are marching, marching by.

Concepts: Shapes (circles)
            Counting
            Quantity (Some, enough, more)

Drawing Circles

(With both arms, make large circles clockwise and counter-clockwise)

Drawing circles!
See my circles:
    Circles in the air!
I'll make some and you make some,
    And we'll have some to spare!

(Make one large circle)
(Make four large circles)

One of them shall be a wheel,
    Although, we may need four!
So, if we don't have quite enough,
    We'll have to make some more!

(Repeat first motions)

Drawing circles!
See my circles:
    Circles in the air!
I'll make some and you make some,
    And we'll have some to spare!

Concepts: Left, right
Numbers

One Hand Left

(Left hand out) **One hand left**
(Right hand out, too)   And one hand right.
(Entwine fingers) Each one held
    The other tight.

(Pull left and back) "Turn me loose!"
    Said the left with a shout.
(Pull right and back) "Help!" said the right;
    "Let me out! Let me out!"

Then, said a voice
    Very soft, very low:
(Slowly relax and release fingers) "One, two, three:
    Relax. Let go."

Concepts: Up, down
Come, go
Seasons of the year
Cause and effect

Smoke Goes Up

(Hands move up slowly) **Smokes goes up**
(Mime raindrops with fingers) And rain comes down
(Move hands together left to right and stop suddenly) And water runs and freezes.

(Push hands away from body) Summer goes
(Bring hands toward body) And winter comes
("cough, cough, cough!") And so do coughs
("kerCHOO!") And sneezes!

Concepts: Body Awareness

Feet and Ankles

(Grasping with both hands)   **Feet and ankles;** legs and knees!
(Show; and touch)   Hands and fingers, arms and sleeves!
    One is not a part of me.
(Teacher says:)   ''Tell me: which one would it be??''

Concepts: Group behavior

Tiptoe, Tiptoe!

(Children may proceed single file; or, in addition, to keep proper distance between each other, each child can place right hand, with arm held straight, on the right shoulder of the child ahead in line.)

Tiptoe, tiptoe!
  Quietly,
I'm the leader:
  Follow me!

Out the door
  And down the hall.
No one hears us:
  Not at all!

Concepts: Body Awareness

I'm Made That Way

(Point to feet with hands, palms up)   If these are my feet,
(Point to toes with forefingers)   Then, those are my toes.
(Put hands to cheeks)   If this is my face,
(Point to nose)   Then, this is my nose.

(Tap head)   If this is my head,
(Take hair in fingers)   Then, this is my hair.
(Point to and blink eyes)   If these are my eyes,
(Hold up two fingers)   Then, I have a pair!

(Pat upper leg)   If this is my leg,
(Take hold of and bend knee)   I'm touching my knee!
(Hand on forearm)   If this is my arm,
(Hold hand up in front of face)   It's MY hand I see!

(Intertwine fingers)   My parts fit together:
(Run hands down sides of body)   **I'm made that way!**
(Start hand low, palm down, and raise to end of rhyme)   And growing a little bit More every day!

Concepts: Left/Right, Both
Eye Dexterity

Wink, Wink, Blink!

Wink with your left eye.
Wink with your right.
Blink, blink, blink!
Then, close them tight!

(Open, then close left eye) Peek with your left eye.
(Open, then close right eye) Peek with your right.
Both eyes closed, now.
Say, "Goodnight!"

(Lay head on hands)

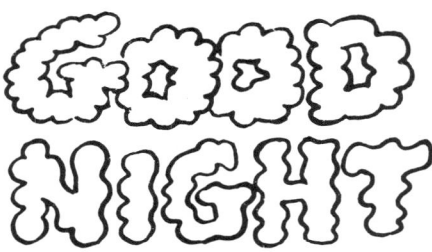